THE HISTORY DETECTIVE INVESTIGATES

VICTORIAN CRIME

Peter Chrisp

HODDER
Wayland

HERRINGTHORPE JUNIOR SCHOOL
CHATTERTON DRIVE
ROTHERHAM

Editor: Kay Barnham
Designer: Simon Borrough
Cartoon artwork: Richard Hook
Picture research: Shelley Noronha – Glass Onion Pictures

First published in Great Britain in 2002 by Hodder Wayland,
an imprint of Hodder Children's Books
© Copyright 2002 Hodder Wayland

Hodder Children's Books
A division of Hodder Headline Limited
338 Euston Road, London NW1 3BH

All rights reserved. No part of this publication may be
reproduced, stored in a retrieval system, or transmitted, in any
form or by any means without the prior written permission of
the publisher, nor be otherwise circulated in any form of binding
or cover other than that in which it is published and without a
similar condition being imposed on the subsequent purchaser.

British Library Cataloguing in Publication Data
Chrisp, Peter
    The history detective investigates Victorian crime
    1. Crime – Great Britain – History – 19th century
    2. Great Britain – Social conditions – 20th century
    I. Title II. Victorian crime
    364.9'41'09034

ISBN 0 7502 3740 6

Printed and bound in Hong Kong

Picture acknowledgements:
The publishers would like to thank the following
for permission to reproduce their pictures:
BEAMISH The North of England Open Air
Museum 14 (right), 16 (right), 17 (bottom-left);
Billie Love Historical Collection 19 (bottom), 23
(top), 25 (bottom), 27 (top), 27 (bottom);
Bridgeman Art Library *cover* (bottom-left, middle,
bottom-right, top-right); John Frost 28; Hulton
Getty 22; Jim Linley/Inverary Jail 27 (right); Mary
Evans Picture Library *cover* (top-left), 1, 4, 5 (left
and right), 7, 8 (bottom), 9, 11, 12 (left and right),
13 (left), 14 (top), 15 (bottom), 17 (top and right),
18 (top-left and top-right), 19 (left), 20 (right), 21,
23 (bottom), 25 (top-left), 26, 29 (top and
bottom); Museum of London *cover* (rattle); Peter
Newark's Pictures 10 (left and right), 13 (bottom),
15 (top), 16, 19 (top-right), 24; Punch 6; Ronald
Grant Archive 8 (top).

CONTENTS

WHAT CAUSED VICTORIAN CRIME?

In the Victorian period, almost everything to do with life in Britain changed. People moved from the countryside to new towns and cities, and the population more than doubled, from 16 million in 1837, to 37 million in 1901. As the number of people rose, so did the number of crimes committed. This rise in crime worried the Victorians. They wondered what caused it, and what they could do about it.

One cause of Victorian crime was poverty (being poor). In every town, there was a slum area, where many people turned to crime in order to live. The picture below shows a slum district of London, nicknamed 'the devil's acre'.

The history detective, Sherlock Bones, will help you to find clues and collect evidence about Victorian crime – why people turned to crime, and how they were caught and punished.

Wherever you see one of Sherlock's paw-prints, like this, you will find a mystery to solve. The answers can all be found on page 31.

❖ Why do you think this part of London was called 'the devil's acre'?

These cartoons both date from September 1888, when the police were trying to catch a murderer, nicknamed Jack the Ripper. He killed five women in the slums of East London, but was never caught.[1]

The cartoon on the right shows crime as a scary phantom, or spirit, rising out of a slum. Its caption begins, 'There floats a phantom on the slum's foul air'.

Middle-class Victorians thought that some people were born to be criminals, and you could spot them from their appearance. Look at the faces of the criminals in the cartoon below. They have wide mouths, small noses and low foreheads – like apes. Look out for other 'criminal faces' in Victorian cartoons.

♣ Why do you think this policeman is wearing a blindfold?

DETECTIVE WORK

One good place to look for clues about Victorian crime is the Internet. Using a search engine, such as www.google.com, type in key words, such as 'Victorian' and the name of the crime you are investigating.

WHO WERE THE 'FAMILY PEOPLE'?

'**F**amily people' was a nickname, used by professional criminals to describe themselves. They were people who lived only by crime, and took pride in their criminal skills. Each type of criminal tended to stick to one sort of crime, such as burglary or picking pockets. However, they felt that they were all members of one big 'family', and looked down on those who obeyed the law as outsiders.

The criminal 'family' had its own secret language, called cant. This allowed criminals to pass on information without letting outsiders know what they were talking about. Here are a few Victorian canting terms. See how many more you can collect.

alderman	a half-crown coin
billy	a silk handkerchief
bull	five shillings
chiv	a knife
crow	a lookout
crusher	policeman
drag	a three-month prison sentence
flying the blue pigeon	stealing lead off roofs
hoisting	shoplifting
in lavender	in hiding from the police
nibbed	arrested
nommus!	get away quick!
stall	a thief's helper who got in the way of pursuers

People who received stolen goods were called 'fences'. Victorian books and pictures often show fences as Jews. This was simply because in slum areas, Jews ran the most successful businesses, such as second-hand clothes shops, and pawnbrokers.

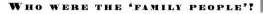

Criminals had their own pubs, called 'flash houses', where they met to plan jobs, and arrange the sale of stolen goods. The engraving above shows a group of criminals meeting in a 'flash house' in Camberwell, South London.

✤ Can you work out what this Victorian thief is talking about? The list of words on page 6 might help you.

'We were *hoisting billies* when our *crow* spotted a *crusher* and shouted '*nommus!*' We would have been *nibbed* too, if the *stall* hadn't tripped the *crusher* up.'

✤ What are the three men in the background doing?

DETECTIVE WORK

You can find lists of Victorian canting terms in slang dictionaries, and on the Internet. Search using words such as 'Victorian', 'cant', 'thieves' and 'slang'. Then try writing your own sentences in thieves' cant!

WHAT CRIMES DID CHILDREN COMMIT?

Professional criminals started at a very young age in Victorian Britain. Small boys worked for burglars as 'little snakesmen'. They would wriggle, like snakes, through barred windows to open the doors of houses from the inside. But the most common crime committed by children was 'dipping', or picking pockets.

Anthony Newley played the Artful Dodger in the film of *Oliver Twist* (David Lean, 1948).

DETECTIVE WORK

Find out as much as you can about child pickpockets. One good source of information is Dickens' *Oliver Twist*. You could read the novel, or look out for the 1948 film of the book, by David Lean, which is available on video.

Because they were small, child pickpockets could walk up to a likely victim in a crowded place without being seen. They were just the right height to lift a handkerchief or a purse from a pocket, and their light fingers meant that they were not likely to be caught in the act.

Child pickpockets worked in gangs, trained and run by adults, called 'kidsmen'. This picture shows a kidsman and two pickpockets.

✿ This description below includes two clues that the Artful Dodger grew up in the slums. What are they?

Charles Dickens describes a dipper, nicknamed the Artful Dodger, in his novel, *Oliver Twist*:
'He was a snub-nosed, flat-browed, common-faced boy… short of his age: with rather bow legs, and little sharp ugly eyes… as swaggering a young gentleman as ever stood four feet six.'

A Transfer of Property.

As they grew older and more skilful, pickpockets could specialise in particular types of robbery. 'Maltoolers', for example, sat on crowded horse-drawn buses, robbing the passengers on either side of them. The jolting of the bus helped hide their movements. The most successful pickpockets belonged to the 'swell mob' – pickpockets who dressed as gentlemen. They did not look like thieves, so they were able to work in crowds without being suspected.

Dippers often worked in pairs, like the two boys in the picture above. The boy on the far left was nicknamed the 'stickman'.

❧ What is the boy on the right trying to do?

❧ What did the stickman do to help the pickpocket?

DID CRIME EVER PAY?

The cracksmen below are very well dressed.

One group of professional criminals was able to make a lot of money. They were called 'cracksmen', a nickname given to burglars and safe-breakers. These were thieves who chose the richest targets to rob, such as stately homes and banks. They could make a lot of money, and often lived and dressed as gentlemen. The most sucessful cracksmen only committed one or two crimes a year, but they would spend months planning them.

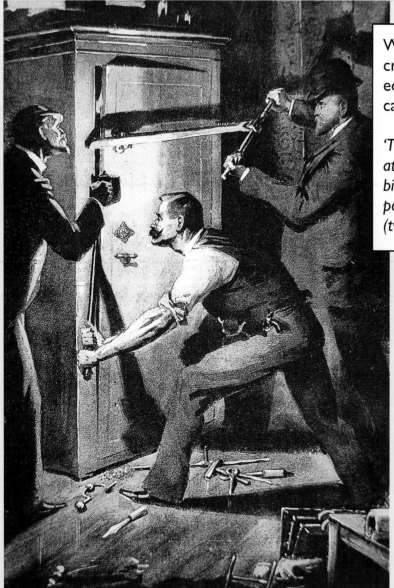

When they went to do a burglary, cracksmen took a bag stuffed with special equipment. In 1839, a prison governor, called G.C.Chesterton listed these items:

'The following are more or less required at every crack (burglary): crow-bar, centre-bit, lantern, keys, picklock, saw, pistol, pocket-knife, nux vomica or prussic acid (two poisons).'

❀ Why do you think burglars needed poison?

Cracksmen needed picklocks and keys to break into houses and safes.

❀ Why do you think it was an advantage for a cracksman to pose as a gentleman?

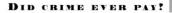

The biggest and most daring robbery of the Victorian period was the 'Great Train Robbery' of 15 May 1855. It was planned by a 39-year-old cracksman, called Edward Agar. With his partner, William Pierce, Agar stole 100kg in gold from the London to Folkestone train. They replaced the gold with an equal weight of lead, for they knew that the gold chests would be weighed at Folkestone, but not opened until they reached Paris, two days after the robbery.

Agar was eventually caught when his girlfriend betrayed him. At his trial, he admitted that he had been a professional thief since he was 18 years old. Yet this was the first time he was ever tried. So, for Edward Agar, crime *did* pay for a while.

Edward Agar, who took part in the 'Great Train Robbery' of 1855.

DETECTIVE WORK

Imagine you are Edward Agar planning to rob a train. List all the problems you would have to solve. What sort of things could go wrong?

WHAT WERE GAROTTERS?

In 1862, Victorian newspapers were full of alarming stories of a new type of violent robbery. It was usually carried out in a dark street by two or three men, one of whom would grab the victim around the neck, choking him, while the others went through his pockets. The name of the crime, invented by the newspapers, was 'garotting'.

✤ This cartoon, from *Punch* magazine, dates from the winter of 1862. What do you think these men are doing?

A gentleman is garotted in a dark street.

The *Times* claimed that there was a 'new rush of crime'. In fact, there had been just as many violent robberies the previous year. What was new in 1862 was that newspaper editors realised that stories about garottings were a good way to sell their papers. They sent journalists out to look for them.

DO YOU WISH TO AVOID BEING STRANGLED!!

If so, try our Patent Antigarotte Collar, which enables Gentlemen to walk the streets of London in perfect safety at all hours of the day or night.

THESE UNIQUE ARTICLES OF DRESS

Are made to measure, of the hardest steel, and are warranted to withstand the grip of

THE MOST MUSCULAR RUFFIAN IN THE METROPOLIS,

Who would get black in the face himself before he could make the slightest impression upon his intended victim. They are highly polished and

Elegantly Studded with the Sharpest Spikes,

Thus combining a most *recherché* appearance with perfect protection from the murderous attacks which occur every day in the most frequented thoroughfares. Price 7s. 6d., or six for 40s.

WHITE, CHOKER, AND Co.

EFFECT OF THE ANTIGAROTTE COLLAR ON A GARROTTEER.

✤ This advertisement for an anti-garotting collar was printed in *Punch*. Do you think it is a serious advertisement?

A poem in *Punch* imagined two anti-garotters meeting in a dark street:

'Is that a footstep behind my back?
It must be one of the strangling pack;
Is that a lurking villain I view,
Crouched in the doorway of number two?…
Where's my revolver? Good gracious! I see
He's bringing his pistol to bear on me!
Hold hard, put up your weapon, Sir, do –
I am an anti-garotter too!'

The press stories led to a widespread panic about crime. Some people became so frightened that they refused to leave their homes after dark. Others formed 'anti-garotting societies' to hunt down garotters. Several innocent men found themselves attacked, or dragged to the police station.

The newspapers made such a fuss about garotting that the government felt that it had to do something. In 1863, a 'Garotters' Act' was passed, which brought in flogging, on top of imprisonment, as a punishment for violent robbery.

DETECTIVE WORK

Many libraries keep copies of Victorian newspapers, such the *Illustrated London News*, and *Punch*. Look out for press stories and cartoons to do with crime. Can you find any that were meant to frighten the readers? Compare them with the way that modern newspapers treat crime. Do we still have 'crime scares' started by the press?

A scene after a flogging at Newgate Prison.

WHY DID MURDERERS USE POISON?

FATAL FACILITY; OR, POISONS FOR THE ASKING.

This cartoon shows a child easily buying poison over the counter.

In the Victorian period, poison was easily available in chemists' shops. Arsenic was sold as a rat poison and used as a coating on fly papers. You could soak these in water to make a poisonous liquid, which could be added to someone's food or drink. At the same time, doctors found it hard to tell if people had been poisoned or died from natural causes. So murderers often used poison as their weapon.

The worst Victorian poisoner was probably Mary Ann Cotton. Between 1852 and 1872, she killed all four of her husbands, along with eight children and step-children. Mary Ann gave them tea with arsenic in it. Her reason for doing this was to collect insurance money. She was only caught, after twenty years of poisoning people, when a local doctor became suspicious of her.

Victorian poison bottle

DETECTIVE WORK

Find out about other famous Victorian poison cases on the Internet. Using a search engine, look up the word 'poison' along with the following names: William Palmer, Madeleine Smith and Florence Maybrick. See if you can find out why these people turned to murder.

The Victorian period saw the launch of the first popular newspapers, aimed at a wide readership. The new papers, such as the *News of the World* and the *Illustrated Police News*, filled their pages with stories of murderers. People were shocked, but could not help being fascinated by these stories.

The cartoon below shows a popular press journalist following a detective as he tries to track down a criminal. The criminal, on the right, is reading all about the police investigation in the 'Muck Rake Gazette'. The cartoon dates from the time of the Jack the Ripper murders, when the police were unable to find the killer.

The front page of this newspaper shows Kate Eddowes, a victim of Jack the Ripper. He was never caught.

✿ What point is the cartoon making?

OCTOBER 20, 1888.]   PUNCH, OR THE LONDON CHARIVARI.   183

IS DETECTION A FAILURE?

WHAT WAS A 'PEELER'?

In the early 1800s, there was no proper police force in Britain. Law and order was left to a few badly paid officials, who worked for the law courts. In times of serious trouble, such as riots, the army was sent in. Then, in 1829, Sir Robert Peel founded the London Metropolitan Police Force, whose members were nicknamed 'bobbies' and 'peelers', after their founder. The new peelers were so successful that, before long, other police forces were set up all over the country.

On duty, a police officer wore a blue coat with brass buttons, blue trousers, and a black top hat. This outfit was more like a Victorian servant's clothes than a military uniform. It was meant to show that a policeman was there to serve the public. Each policeman carried a wooden truncheon, handcuffs and a rattle, used to call for help.

A wooden truncheon

'The lads endeavour to take the unsuspecting "crusher" by surprise, and often crouch at the entrance of a court until a policeman passes, when a stone or brick is hurled at him.'
Henry Mayhew, London Labour and the London Poor

❧ Can you think of any reasons why policemen wore top hats?

The purpose of the police was both to catch criminals and to prevent crimes happening. They did this by patrolling the streets, walking at a steady pace. During one shift, a policeman might walk 40 kilometres.

The police were very unpopular in slum areas, where they were nicknamed 'crushers'. Poor people thought they were only there to protect the rich.

❧ Why do you think the police started wearing helmets instead of top hats?

DETECTIVE WORK

The West Midlands Police Museum has a wonderful website on Victorian police. It has photographs of policemen and criminals, recruiting adverts, and newspaper reports on trials. You can find it at: http://www.stvincent.ac.uk/Resources/WMidPol/main.html

Police often patrolled slum areas in twos or threes, as they feared they would be attacked.

WHAT WAS IT LIKE TO BE ARRESTED AND TRIED?

When a criminal was 'nibbed' or arrested, he or she was taken to the nearest police station and charged with the crime. The next stage was to appear before a 'beak', or magistrate, a part-time, unpaid judge. Magistrates had the power to try and sentence people for minor crimes, such as shoplifting. If the crime was serious, the magistrate would order the prisoner to be tried in a criminal court. Here the decision was made by a jury and the sentence was passed down by a judge in a white wig.

Victorian magistrates were usually wealthy upper-class men. Women had few rights. They were not allowed to be judges, lawyers, or to sit on juries.

A criminal trial was a contest between two lawyers, one arguing that the accused was guilty, while the other argued the opposite. At the end of the trial, the judge summed up the case made by each lawyer, to help the jurymen make up their minds.

**A Victorian lawyer –
Henry Bodkin Poland.**

**A Victorian judge –
Sir Charles Edward Pollock.**

DETECTIVE WORK

There are several sites about Florence Maybrick's trial on the Internet. You may also be able to find books about famous trials in the crime section of your local library. Choose a particular crime and write speeches for the lawyers on each side to make. Then write the judge's summing up.

Photography, a Victorian invention, was used to take pictures of criminals in the police station. These engravings, based on police photographs, show criminals who did not want to be photographed!

The cartoon above shows a rich man and a poor man appearing before a magistrate. The rich man goes free, after paying a fine. The poor man cannot afford to pay and will be sent to prison.

The picture below shows Mrs Florence Maybrick, on trial for poisoning her husband in 1889. The jury of middle-class men sits on the right. The judge looks down from his high seat.

☙ How might the look of someone on trial influence the jury?

☙ Why is Mrs Maybrick wearing a black dress?

WHAT WAS 'BEING STRETCHED'?

Being stretched' was the nickname for death by hanging, the penalty for murder. Until 1868, murderers were hanged in public, in front of crowds of onlookers. This was to make people think about the terrible punishment awaiting criminals. They were supposed to go away with more respect for the law.

Charles Dickens

Public hangings drew vast crowds, especially if the murderers were well known. In 1849, Frederick Manning and his wife Maria were hanged outside Horsemonger Lane Prison, London. Their murder case was so famous that 30,000 people came to watch them die.

In the middle of the crowd was the writer Charles Dickens. He was shocked by the hangings, but even more upset by the behaviour of the crowd. He wrote that he was surrounded by 'thieves' and 'ruffians' who showed 'indecent delight'. Dickens was so upset that, for some time afterwards, he felt as if he was 'living in a city of devils'.

An excited crowd watches a hanging outside Newgate Prison.

This picture shows the hanging of Louise Masset inside Newgate Prison in 1900. She was the first person to be hanged in the 20th century and one of the last of the Victorian era.

✿ Why did pickpockets do well at hangings?

DETECTIVE WORK
From 1868, executions were held in private, inside prisons. Make a list of the reasons why the government might have decided to stop hanging people in public.

A pickpocket who was at the hangings of Frederick and Maria Manning later described his day's takings:

'Mrs Manning was dressed beautiful when she came up... I did four shillings sixpence at the hanging — two handkerchiefs, and a purse with 2 shillings in it — the best purse I ever had.'

WHY WERE PRISONS OVERCROWDED?

A scene from Newgate Prison.

In the early 1800s, there was a big rise in the number of criminals being sent to prison. This was partly due to the rise in crime and also because of better ways of catching criminals. Another reason was that, before 1837, hanging had been the punishment for over 200 different crimes. The Victorians got rid of hanging for everything except murder. This meant that people who would once have been hanged now had to be sent to prison.

This picture shows Newgate, one of the old prisons, in 1800. The prisoners, including men, women, and children, were allowed to mix freely with each other. Newgate was not meant to be a place to punish criminals, but to hold them while they awaited trial or punishment. The real punishments were being hanged, flogged, or transported (shipped to Australia).

Convicts were also kept on old disused warships, called hulks, which were moored off navy bases at Woolwich, Portsmouth and Deptford. In the daytime, the convicts, who each wore a 14-pound (6.4 kg) leg-iron, came ashore to work in the dockyards. They spent their nights on board the hulks, which were dirty, disease-ridden and overcrowded.

The hulks were only meant to be a short-term answer for what to do with convicts, while enough new prisons could be built to take them. Like Newgate, hulks were thought to be places that encouraged crime. First offenders and children found themselves surrounded by hardened criminals.

DETECTIVE WORK
Read the beginning of Charles Dickens' novel, *Great Expectations*. It starts with a convict called Magwitch escaping from a hulk.

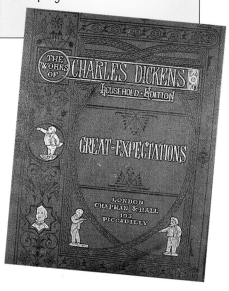

'His time is passed in the midst of a body of criminals of every class… He returns a greater adept (expert) in crime… and… is generally known to all the worst men in the country.'
Parliamentary Report, 1836

❧ Why did the convicts wear leg-irons?

❧ How can you tell that this ship is no longer used for sailing?

A prison hulk

What was 'Getting the Boat'?

One answer to the problem of what to do with convicts was to send them half-way around the world to Australia. This was called transportation and was nicknamed 'getting the boat'. Transportation lasted from 1787 and 1868. In this period, around 160,000 British men, women and children were shipped to Australia.

The voyage to Australia took six months, with prisoners locked below deck in cages for most of the time.

One reason to transport convicts was simply to get rid of them, so that they would no longer be able to commit crimes in Britain. Another reason was that the government wanted to turn Australia into a British colony, and settlers were needed to build towns and farm the land. Prisoners were forced to work in prison camps and for free settlers. Once they had finished their sentence, they could become free settlers themselves.

How would you feel to be separated from your friends and family, and sent to the other side of the world? For the convicts, used to life in Victorian Britain, being transported to Australia was like being sent to another planet.

✤ In 1851, gold was discovered in Australia. Do you think this changed people's attitude to being transported?

Successful gold diggers celebrate in Australia.

Many convicts wrote letters home to their families. This one was written by a man called Henry Tingley to his parents:

'We have as much to eat as we like… All a man has to do is to keep a still tongue in his head, and do his master's duty… but if he don't, he may as well be hung at once, for they would take you to the magistrates and get 100 lashes… I am doing a great deal better than ever I was at home, only the wanting you with me'

LAST OF THE CONVICT SHIPS
OVER ONE HUNDRED YEARS OLD
RAISED FROM THE BOTTOM OF SIDNEY HARBOUR
ONCE SEEN NEVER FORGOTTEN.

The last convict ship, opened to the public in the early 1900s.

DETECTIVE WORK

Find out about what life was like on board a convict ship, and what happened to the convicts once they reached Australia. One good place to look for clues is the *Convicts to Australia* website. You can find it at: http://www.convictcentral.com/index.html

WHAT WAS THE 'SEPARATE SYSTEM'?

In 1842, the first of the new Victorian prisons opened, at Pentonville in London. It was designed to try out a new way of dealing with convicts, called the 'separate system'. Pentonville was built to hold around 500 male convicts, who were kept apart from each other in separate cells. The idea was to stop prisoners being a bad influence on each other. By 1850, fifty-four new prisons had been built, modelled on Pentonville.

The convicts' only human contact was with the guards and the prison chaplain, who talked to them about God. It was hoped that the prisoners, forced to think about religion, would reform, or turn to a better way of life.

The only time prisoners saw each other at Pentonville was in the exercise yard. The men in this picture all wear identical uniforms and masks.

🐾 Why do you suppose the prisoners had to wear masks?

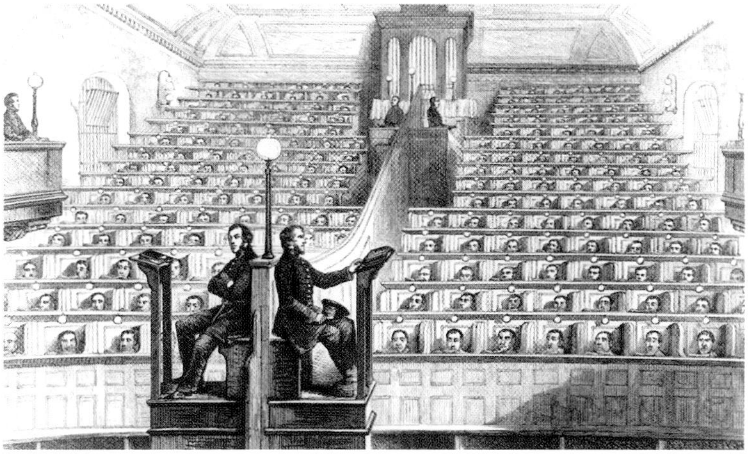

Even the prison chapel was designed to follow the 'separate system', with the prisoners boxed off from each other.

By the 1850s, the idea that prisoners could be reformed had gone out of fashion. Convicts released from Pentonville often went straight back to crime. The aim of late Victorian prisons was not to reform criminals, but to punish them. Life in a prison was designed to be as unpleasant as possible, in the hope that criminals would never want to go back there.

One prison punishment was the 'treadmill' – a great revolving drum, which the convicts turned by climbing its steps. This was like being trapped in a machine. Another was turning a 'crank' – a metal drum, filled with sand. In one day, a prisoner was expected to turn his crank 10,000 times. If he refused, he would be whipped or put on a diet of bread and water.

What was the point of turning a crank or a treadmill?

Convicts climbing the never-ending steps of a treadmill.

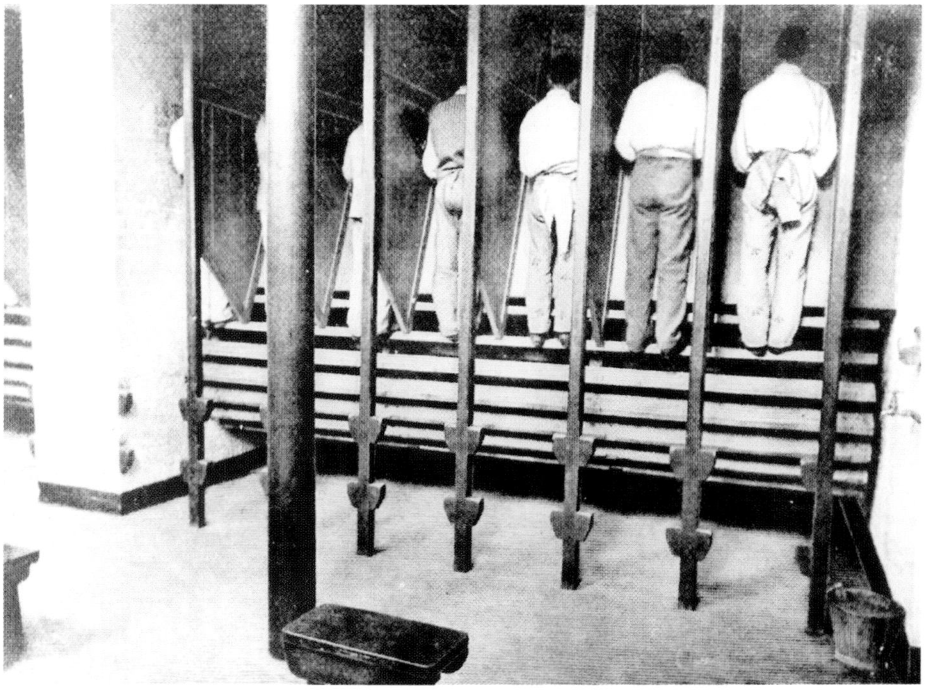

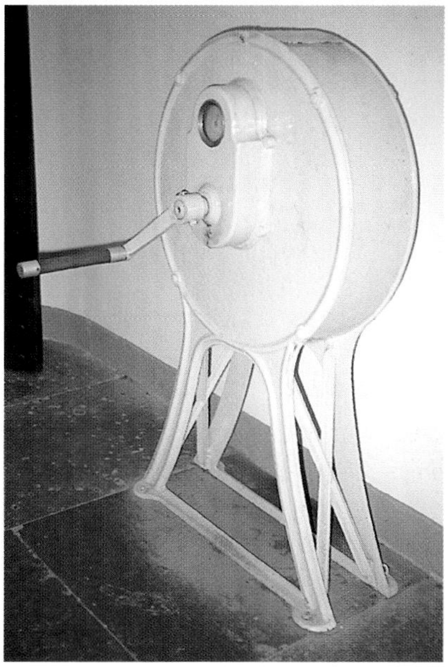

The crank at Inverary Museum

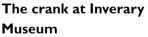

Detective work

Britain has several prison museums, including Inverary Jail, Ripon Prison, Lincoln Castle, and the Prison Service Museum, Rugby. If you get the chance, visit one of these to find out what life was like for a Victorian prisoner.

Your Project

By now, you should have collected enough clues to put together your own project about Victorian crime. Now is the time to think about what sort of a project you want to produce.

The first thing to do is to choose a topic to investigate. You might decide to look at a particular type of crime, such as burglary, or a punishment, such as transportation. You might want to look at the crimes that were committed in the area where you live. Remember that it's your project, so choose something you find interesting.

A front page from 1888, showing bloodhounds on the trail of Jack the Ripper.

Why not pick something unusual as your topic? Sherlock Bones has been finding out about Victorian police dogs. He's discovered that, in October 1888, the police used two bloodhounds, called Barnaby and Burgho, to try to track down the murderer nicknamed Jack the Ripper. They were taken to the crime scenes, but were unable to follow the scent of the killer.

Looking through the newspapers, Sherlock found several letters about the bloodhounds. On 3 October 1888, a dog lover called Percy Linley wrote to the Pall Mall Gazette praising the bloodhound for his *'keen scent, quick intelligence, patience, and power of concentration … to say nothing of his good looks.'* Linley concluded, *'The London police will find a good friend in the bloodhound, given patience to train him in the way he should go.'*

✤ A bloodhound from the Jack the Ripper investigation appears somewhere else in this book. Can you find him?

Project Presentation

- Put together your own Victorian newspaper, with articles, pictures, cartoons and letters from the public.
- Imagine that you are a Victorian police detective investigating a crime. Assemble a police file with cuttings, evidence, and your own police reports.
- Write a policeman's notebook, recording a day on the beat in a Victorian slum district.
- Write a diary of a day in a Victorian prison.

A Victorian slum district, where poverty often drove people to commit crime.

Victorian policemen breaking up a violent riot in Hyde Park, London.

GLOSSARY

arsenic A poison used to kill rats, flies, and murder victims.

cant Secret language used by Victorian criminals.

convict Someone found guilty of a crime, and sentenced to prison, or transportation.

cracksman Burglar or safe-breaker.

dipper A pickpocket.

family people Members of the Victorian professional criminal class.

fence Receiver of stolen goods.

hulk A disused warship, used as a prison.

insurance Money paid out on death, injury, or loss. When a man died, his widow would collect this, if he had previously taken out a policy with an insurance company.

jury A group of twelve men who made the decision of guilt or innocence in a criminal trial.

magistrate An unpaid, part-time judge.

peeler Nickname of a policeman, after Sir Robert Peel. They were also called 'bobbies', 'coppers' and 'crushers'.

separate system Prison system in which prisoners were not allowed to see any other prisoners. They spent most of their time alone in a cell.

transportation The shipping of convicts to Australia, where they were forced to work.

ANSWERS

page 4: ✤ It was called the 'devil's acre' because it was thought to be a place of wickedness, where people grew up to be criminals. The name also suggests that this was a hellish place to have to live.

page 5: ✤ The policeman is blindfolded to show the difficulties that the police were having in finding Jack the Ripper. The police seemed to be losing in the battle against crime.

page 7: ✤ Cant translation: We were shoplifting silk handkerchiefs when our lookout spotted a policeman, and shouted, 'Get away quick!' We would have been arrested too, if our helper hadn't tripped him up.'

✤ The man on the right is keeping watch for policemen, through a hole in the door. The man on the left is a thief, trying to sell stolen goods to the Jewish 'fence'. The 'fence' raises his hands, perhaps showing how impressed he is with the goods; or perhaps he is saying, 'you're asking too high a price!'

page 8: ✤ The Artful Dodger's short height is a sign of poverty and a bad diet. Wealthier Victorians were noticeably taller than the poor, because they ate better food. Bow legs are another sign of a slum background. They were caused by rickets – twisted bone growth caused by bad food and a lack of sunlight.

page 9: ✤ The boy is learning to be a pickpocket. He is trying to lift a handkerchief from a suit hung with bells. A skilled pickpocket could do this without making the bells ring.

✤ The 'stickman' was secretly passed the stolen wallet or handkerchief by the pickpocket. If the pickpocket was then caught, he could show that he had no stolen property on him.

page 10: ✤ Burglars gave poisoned meat to dogs in the houses they robbed, to stop them barking.

The police would not think that a man dressed as a gentleman was a criminal. By dressing like this, a burglar could also look over places he planned to rob without raising suspicion.

page 12: These men are walking back-to-back so that they can keep a lookout for garotters – in all directions!

page 13: It is a joke. Collars like this only existed in cartoons.

page 15: The journalist shines a light on the detective's work, making it public knowledge by printing it in his newspaper. The criminal can then read about how the police investigation is going. The cartoon is saying that newspapers helped criminals to escape arrest.

page 17: The top hat was worn by gentlemen, so it was a sign of respectability. It was worn by policemen to win respect in working class areas where nobody else wore them. It also made the officer look taller, and it helped people recognise a policeman when they needed one.

The top hat was easily knocked off by stone-throwing boys. Helmets gave much better protection in a fight or a riot.

page 19: People who were shabbily dressed and who had 'criminal faces', like those in the cartoons in this book, were more likely to be found guilty by juries. The juries were made up of middle-class men, who would often favour defendants who looked like themselves.

Florence wears black as a sign that she is in mourning – a state of sorrow following the death of her husband, whom she was accused of murdering. She hoped that this would make her look innocent in the jury's eyes.

page 21: Pickpockets liked hangings because there was a big crowd. The people jostled each other, and their whole attention was fixed on the hanging. They did not notice their pockets being picked.

page 23: The leg-irons made it harder to escape, either by swimming away from the hulk at night, or running off from the dockyard in the daytime.

The ship has had its masts cut down, and new buildings built on the deck.

page 25: The discovery of gold in Australia made poor people want to go there, to get rich. To those living in Victorian slums, transportation no longer seemed like a punishment.

page 26: The masks stopped the prisoners recognising each other. This was to stop them getting to know one another in prison, and also to prevent them meeting up again after their release.

page 27: There was no point to turning a crank or a treadmill. The fact that they were pointless made them a harsher punishment. Convicts could not even comfort themselves with the thought that they were doing something useful.

page 28: The bloodhound appears in the cartoon 'Is Detection a Failure?' on page 13. He is probably Barnaby or Burgho.

Books to read

Victorian Law and Order by Andrew Evans (Batsford, 1988)
Victorians by Anne Kramer (Dorling Kindersley, 1998)
Crime and Detection by Brian Lane (Dorling Kindersley, 1998)
Crime and Punishment by Fiona MacDonald (Watts, 1995)

Index